The Universe

Emily Kington

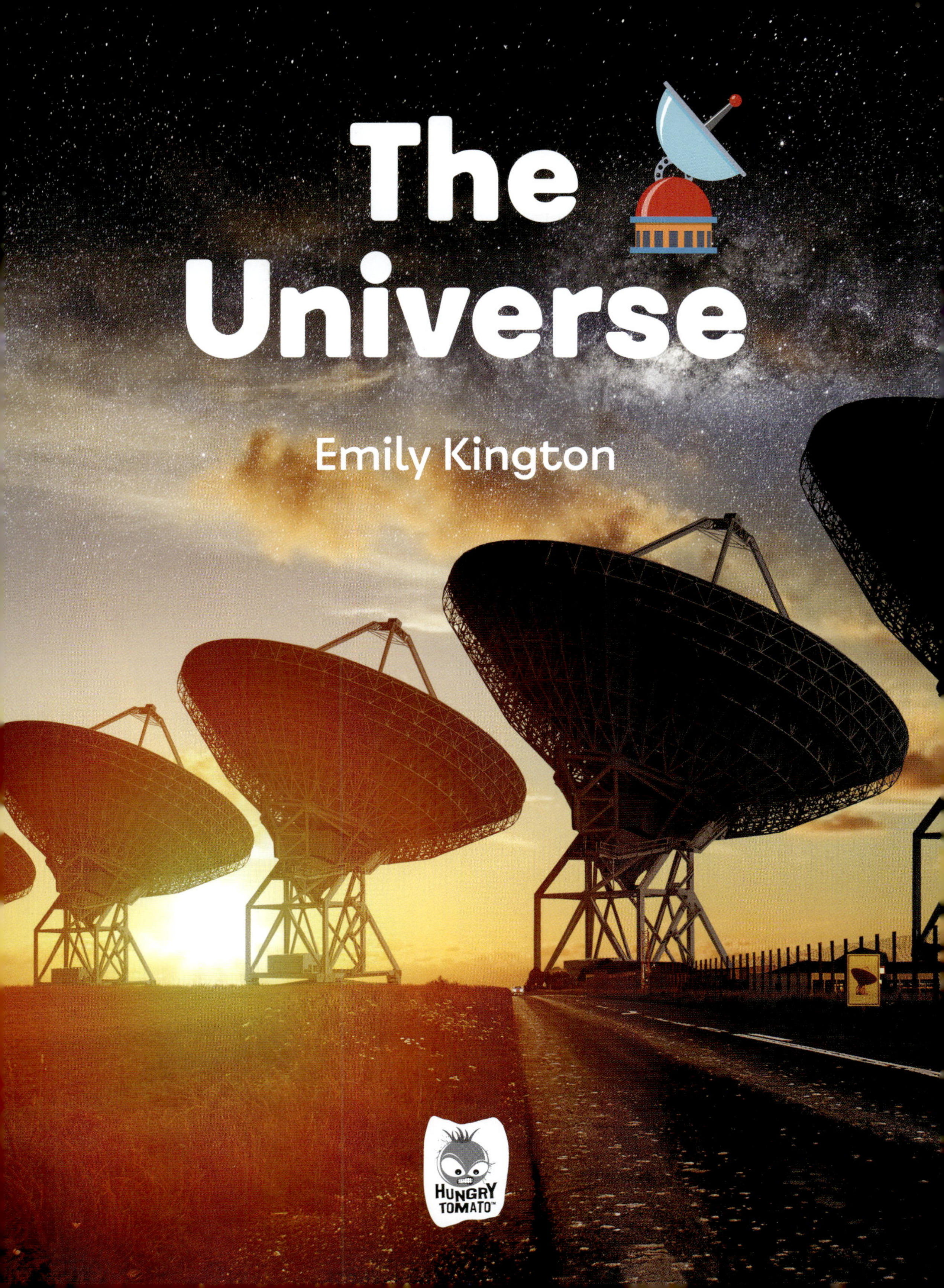

Contents

Words that appear in **bold** are explained in the glossary

Discover more at **www.hungrytomato.com**

What is the Universe?

The Universe is the whole of space and everything that exists within it. Scientists believe that it is getting bigger all the time.

It's not just planets, stars and dust clouds that make up the Universe. All living things on Earth, including every plant that grows, is part of it too!

It is impossible to know how big the Universe actually is. It is so big that we will never be able to discover it all.

The Universe is thought to be more than 13 billion years old!

Many scientists believe that the Universe was created by a massive explosion known as the *Big Bang*.

Our Place in the Universe

Our home planet, Earth, is a very tiny part of the Universe. Earth is part of the **solar system**, which is a small part of a galaxy, known as the *Milky Way*.

Just as Earth spins round the Sun, our solar system spins around the center of our galaxy.

NASA's satellite TESS is searching the Milky Way Galaxy for planets outside of our solar system.

There are thousands of other stars in our galaxy with other planets that **orbit** them.

Our galaxy is called the *Milky Way* because the Romans thought it looked like a milky patch in the night sky.

Galaxies

A galaxy is a huge collection of dust, **gas**, stars and solar systems that are all held together by **gravity**.

There are about 30 other galaxies in our "local" neighbourhood. This is *Andromeda*, the nearest major galaxy to the Milky Way.

In 1924, Astronomer *Edwin Hubble* announced his discovery that the Milky Way was just one of many galaxies.

There could be as many as 100 billion galaxies, but we need more powerful telescopes to see them.

The *Hubble Space Telescope* is able to capture pictures of faraway galaxies and has helped to uncover many mysteries about space.

Stars

A star is a giant ball of very hot gas called *plasma*, which is held together by its own gravity. There are hundreds of billions of stars in the Milky Way.

There are many different types of star. *Red Dwarfs* are the most common kind. They are smaller and cooler than our Sun.

The nearest star to Earth is the Sun, which is a *Yellow Dwarf*.

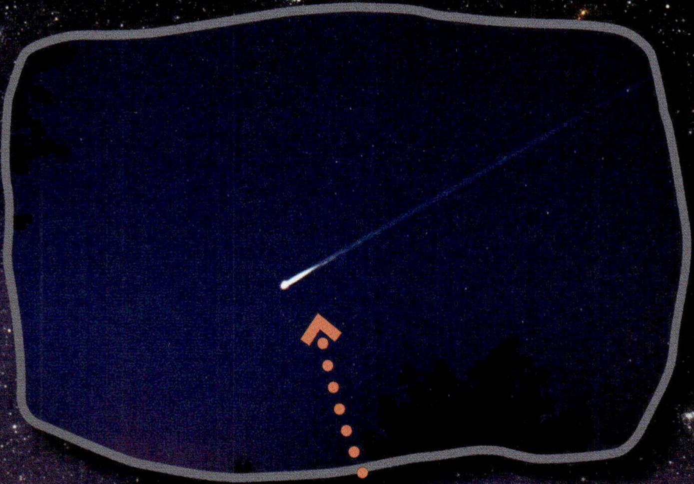

Shooting stars aren't stars at all! They are tiny bits of dust and rock, called *meteoroids, which* burn up as they enter **Earth's atmosphere.**

The largest known star, *VY Canis Majoris*, is over 1,800 times bigger than the Sun!

How long a star lives depends on size. The larger the star, the shorter its life. A star like our Sun lives for about 10 billion years!

The Night Sky

There is lots to discover about space without leaving Earth. For centuries, stargazers and astronomers have studied the stars that we can see in the night sky.

Constellations are groups of bright stars that stand out in the night sky. When joined up like dot-to-dots, they form different shapes.

This constellation is named *Orion*, after a great hunter from Greek myths. It looks a bit like someone holding a bow and arrow.

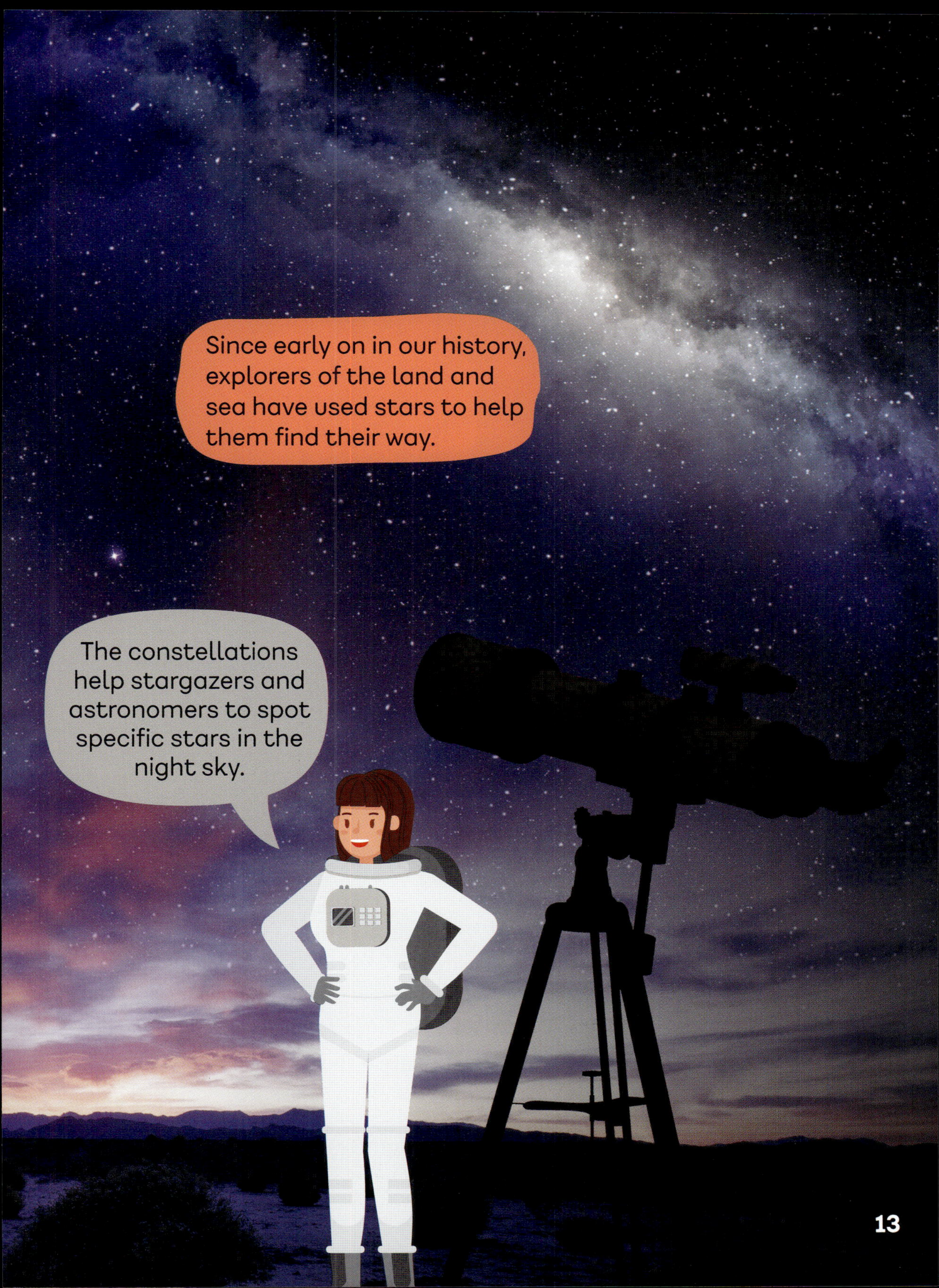

Since early on in our history, explorers of the land and sea have used stars to help them find their way.

The constellations help stargazers and astronomers to spot specific stars in the night sky.

Asteroids

Asteroids are rocky objects, which are much smaller than planets, but also orbit the Sun.

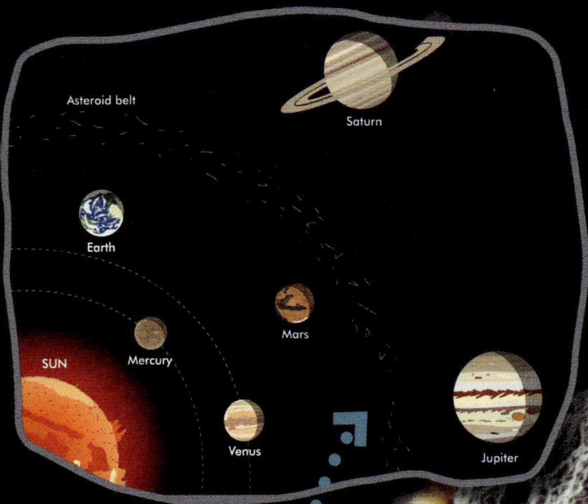

These rocks are leftover from the formation of our solar system.

Most asteroids are found in an area between the orbits of Mars and Jupiter, known as an *asteroid belt.*

Sometimes asteroids come close to Earth. These are called *Near-Earth Objects.*

Asteroids can be as huge as 329 miles (530 km) across or as small as 33 feet (10 meters).

Comets

Comets are space snowballs! They are made from ice, rock, dust and gases. Like asteroids, they also orbit the Sun.

Some comets are up to 15 times bigger than Earth!

Comets can sometimes be seen from Earth. When they get closer to the Sun, their ice and dust boils, which causes them to glow and makes them look like they have a tail.

The most famous comet is probably *Halley's Comet*, which can be seen from Earth every 74–76 years.

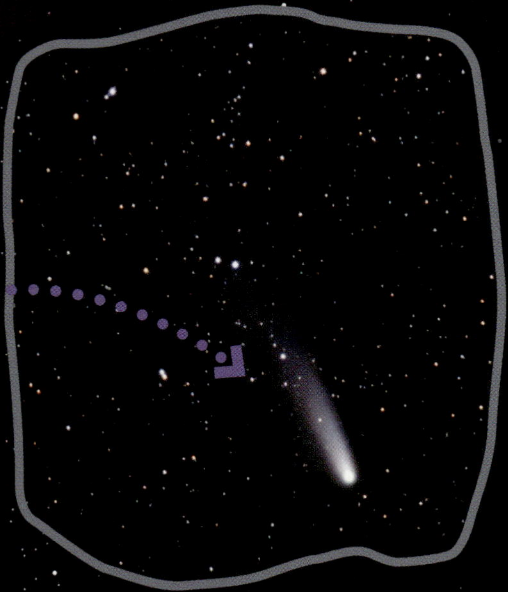

Get this in your diary, Halley's Comet will return sometime in the year 2061.

Black Holes

Even without seeing one, astronomers know that black holes exist because of the effect they have on objects that get close to them.

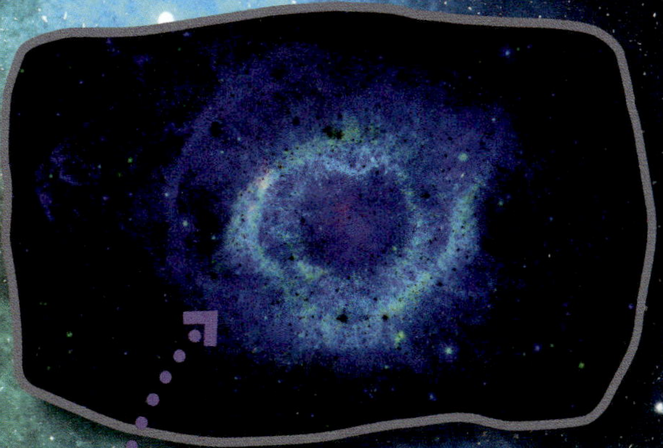

Most black holes are born when a giant star runs out of energy. The star collapses under its own weight, which causes an explosion called a *supernova*.

A black hole's gravity is so strong that it will pull in anything that gets too close, including light!

In 2019, scientists were able to capture an image of a black hole for the first time.

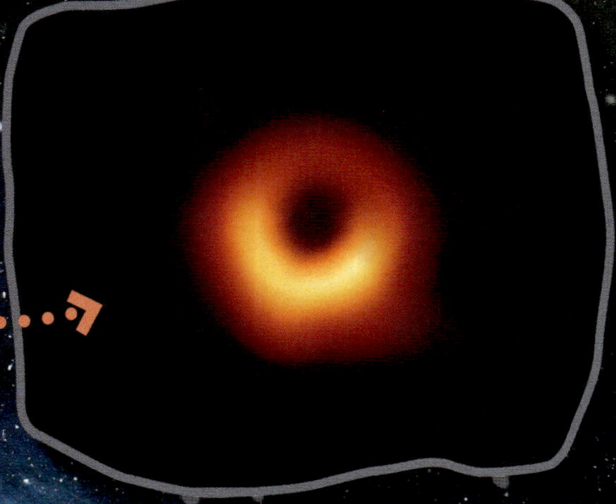

Black Holes are one of the great mysteries in our universe. There is a lot we still don't know about them.

Nebulae

A nebula is a giant cloud of dust and gas in space! They are sometimes created from the dust thrown out by a supernova.

Some **nebulae** are known as "star nurseries", because they are where new stars are born!

One of the brightest is the *Orion Nebula*. It can sometimes be seen in the night sky.

Some nebulae, like the *Eagle Nebula*, form strange, alien-looking shapes.

Meteoroids

Small pieces of rock that travel through space are called *meteoroids*. If they enter a planet's atmosphere and burn up, they are then known as *meteors*.

When lots of meteors fall at once, we call it a *meteor shower*. About 30 meteor showers can be seen from Earth every year.

Meteor showers happen when Earth travels through a stream of dust and rocks left by a passing comet.

Most meteors burn away completely before they can reach Earth's surface. Space rocks that make it are called *meteorites*.

Most meteorites are small rocks or pebbles. The largest meteorite found on Earth is the *Hoba meteorite* in Namibia.

Glossary

Earth's atmosphere – layers of gases around the Earth, held in place by gravity.

gas - a substance that is neither solid or liquid and has no fixed shape. Many gases are invisible.

gravity - a pulling force that works across space. It's the same force that causes an object to fall when you drop it.

nebulae – is the plural name for nebula.

orbit - the path taken by one object circling around another object in space.

solar system – the solar system contains all of the planets, dwarf planets, moons, and other objects that travel around the Sun.

Picture Credits
(abbreviations: t = top; b = bottom; m = middle; l = left; r = right; bg = background)

Shutterstock: Ad_hominem 12l; Antares_StarExplorer 21tl; BJ Nartker 11tr; Blue bee 14l; Brian Donovan 17r; d3verro 1tr, 3t, 4t, 6tr, 8t, 12tr, 14t, 16t, 22t; Dabarti CGI 14bg; Dotted Yeti 7tr, 9b; Ingaav 6bg; Jurik Peter 10bg; Love the wind 4l; Maximilian Laschon 19tr; Mohamed; Elkhamisy 8bg, 21br; NASA images 18l; Paul Fleet 16bg; paulista 12bg; Pike-28 20bg; Rostasedlacek 23br; sdecoret 1bg; SKY2020 22m; Sunflowerr 6m; Vadim Sadovski 2bg, 4bg, 22bg, 24bg; vchal 18bg; VikiVector 10t, 19t, 20t; Yindee (astronaut cartoons).

Every effort has been made to trace the copyright holders and we apologise in advance for any unintentional omissions. We would be pleased to insert the appropriate acknowledgement in any subsequent edition of this publication.

First published in Great Britain in 2021 by Hungry Tomato Ltd
F1, Old Bakery Studios, Blewetts Wharf, Malpas Road, Truro, Cornwall, TR1 1QH, UK

A CIP catalog record for this book is available from the British Library

ISBN 978 1 913440 57 2